I love reading

Flying Giants

by Monica Hughes

Consultant: Luis M. Chiappe, Ph.D.
Director of the Dinosaur Institute
Natural History Museum of Los Angeles County

BEARPORT
PUBLISHING

NEW YORK, NEW YORK

Credits

Cover, Title Page, 10–11, 14–15, 16–17, 18–19, 20, 21, 22, 23B, 24: Luis Rey; 4–5, 6: Natural History Museum; 7: Philip Hood; 8–9, 12: Lisa Alderson; 13: Simon Mendez; 23T: Shutterstock.

Every effort has been made by ticktock Entertainment Ltd. to trace copyright holders. We apologize in advance for any omissions. We would be pleased to insert the appropriate acknowledgments in any subsequent edition of this publication.

Library of Congress Cataloging-in-Publication Data

Hughes, Monica.
Flying giants / by Monica Hughes.
p. cm. — (I love reading. Dino world!)
Includes bibliographical references and index.
ISBN-13: 978-1-59716-541-9 (library binding)
ISBN-10: 1-59716-541-7 (library binding)
1. Pterosauria—Juvenile literature. 2. Pteranodon—Juvenile literature. 3. Birds, Fossil—Juvenile literature. I. Title.

QE862.P7H84 2008
567.918—dc22

2007017665

2 Orchard Business Centre, North Farm Road, Tunbridge Wells, Kent, TN2 3XF, UK

Published in the United States of America by Bearport Publishing Company, Inc.

For more information, write to Bearport Publishing Company, Inc., 101 Fifth Avenue, Suite 6R, New York, New York 10003. Printed in the United States of America.

10 9 8 7 6 5 4 3 2 1

Contents

Flying giants

Pterosaurs were flying animals that lived at the time of the dinosaurs.

Pteranodon
(terr-*an*-oh-DON)

Pterosaur means "flying lizard."

Many of these animals looked like lizards with wings.

The Pterosaurs

(TERR-uh-sorz)

Some pterosaurs were very small.

Others had **wingspans** the size of a small plane—40 feet (12 m) long.

They ate fish, bugs, and **shellfish**.

Sordes
(SOR-dees)

Their light wings helped them make long flights.

Sordes

(SOR-dees)

This pterosaur's wingspan was about as wide as an open picture book.

Sordes had small, sharp teeth.

It ate mainly insects.

Its body had fur to keep it warm.

Eudimorphodon

(*yoo*-dye-MOR-foh-don)

Eudimorphodon was also a pterosaur.

It had about 114 teeth.

Humans have 32 teeth.

Eudimorphodon's teeth helped it catch and eat fish.

Dimorphodon

(dye-MOR-foh-don)

This pterosaur had a huge mouth and two kinds of teeth.

Dimorphodon had a 4-foot (1.2-m) wingspan.

That span is about the length of a golf club.

Dimorphodon probably ate fish.

Pterodactylus

(*terr*-oh-DAK-til-uhss)

This pterosaur lived near the ocean.

Pterodactylus had a long **beak** to help it catch fish.

It had three claws on each wing.

Many other pterosaurs also had claws.

Dsungaripterus

(*jung*-gah-RIP-ter-uhss)

This pterosaur's open wings were as wide as a sofa.

It had a **crest** that ran down the middle of its face.

It probably ate fish and shellfish.

crest

Quetzalcoatlus

(*kwet*-zal-koh-AHT-lus)

This pterosaur is the largest flying animal ever found.

Its wingspan was about 40 feet (12 m).

Many buses are not that long!

It lived near lakes.

It probably ate shellfish and other animals.

Archaeopteryx

(ar-kee-OP-tur-iks)

Archaeopteryx was the first bird.

It was not a pterosaur.

It had feathers.

Unlike today's birds, it had teeth.

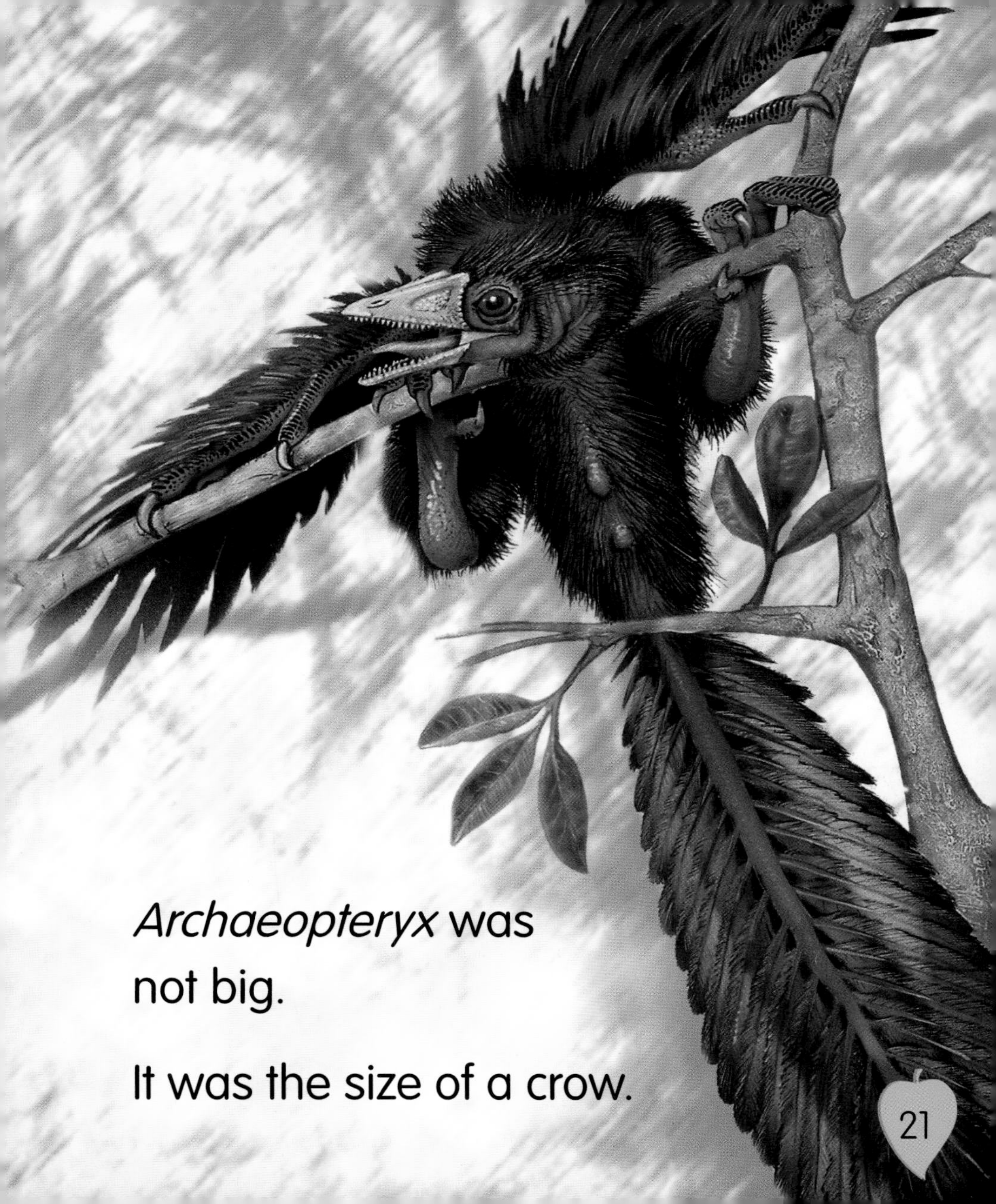

Archaeopteryx was
not big.

It was the size of a crow.

Glossary

beak (BEEK)
the hard, horn-shaped part of an animal's mouth

crest (KREST)
feathers or skin on top of an animal's head

shellfish (SHEL-*fish*)
sea creatures with a shell, such as mussels or clams

wingspans
(WING-*spanz*)
distances between the tips of wings

Index

Read More

Lessem, Don. *Flying Giants of Dinosaur Time.* Minneapolis, MN: Lerner Publications (2005).

Wynne, Patricia J. *Feathered Dinosaurs: Flying Reptiles and Ancient Birds.* Mineola, NY: Dover Publications (2005).

Learn More Online

To learn more about the world of dinosaurs, visit **www.bearportpublishing.com/ILoveReading**